65/2096&97MD

Behold, A Savior!

Songs & Stories of His Birth

Jay Rouse
Rose Aspinall

Editor: Chrislyn Reed
Music Engraving: David Thibodeaux
Cover Design: Ashley Donahue

MEDALLION MUSIC

A Word from the Writers

We are delighted to bring *Behold, A Savior!* to you—delighted. We are story-tellers; Jay with his piano, Rose with her pen. Our hope is that what we set down on paper, be it words or musical notations, will have a life beyond our vision

We always strive to be servants of the work. This creative act is our annunciation. In this way, we keep Jesus alive in our hearts. But once we send it out into the world, it's yours. It no longer depends on our piano and pen. It depends on you. We give this to you with a prayer. May He be born in you. May you become ever more alive in Him. And then, tell the story, His story and your story. Tell it in your own way. Tell it again and again and again.

- *Jay and Rose*

Index

Joy to the World!

Words by
ISAAC WATTS

Music by
JAY ROUSE and
GEORGE FREDERICK HANDEL
Arr. by Jay Rouse

Optional Opening: Today, we have an opportunity to enter the Christmas story in a unique way. We will hear the promises from the scriptures. We will see their fulfillment in the firsthand stories of those who lived them. In each of these stories and songs we will witness some of the events that led up to the birth of the Messiah, the Christ. The world had waited for so long. Now, at last, the fullness of time had arrived. Jesus was the Word made flesh. He came and He dwelt among us. Now witness the irresistible love of the Father for His people. Joy to the world! The Lord is come!

Joy to the world! The Lord is come. Let earth re-ceive her

King._____ Let ev-'ry heart pre-pare Him room and

8

While fields and floods, rocks, hills, and plains re-

peat___ the sound-ing joy,_____ re - peat___ the sound-ing

joy._____ No more let

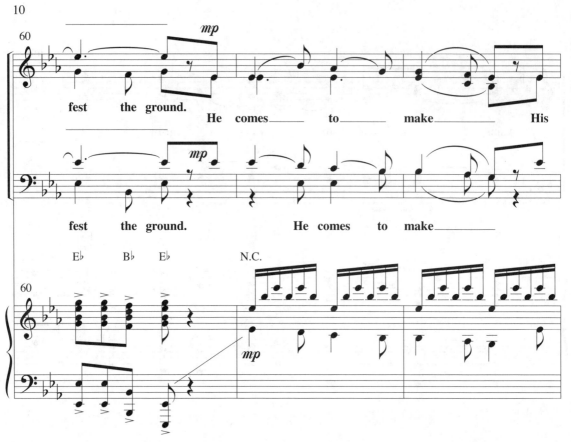

found. He rules the world with truth and grace and makes the na - tions prove the glo - ries of His righ - teous - ness and won - ders of His

The Promise (optional reading):

The beginning of the gospel of Jesus Christ, the Son of God. As it is written in Isaiah the prophet, "Behold, I send My messenger before Your face, who will prepare Your way; The voice of one crying in the wilderness, 'Make ready the way of the Lord, make His paths straight.'" (Mark 1:1-3)

The angel said to him, "Don't be afraid, Zechariah! God has heard your prayer. Your wife Elizabeth will have a son, and you will name him John." (Luke 1:13)

The Fulfillment:

Zechariah: What shall we say of Him? This God of Israel—the God of our Fathers? Just this—that Yahweh will do what Yahweh will do. Now, answer this. When have we needed Messiah more than now, hmm? And what shall we say of this old man, this priest of the division of Abijah!? This—that in the winter of my years I hold the promise of God! Listen, I'll tell you how it happened.

The day before Sabbath, I traveled to Jerusalem to assume my sacred duties. It is as I've always done. The lots were cast and the honor to offer incense in the Holy Place fell to me! Never before had I been selected! Never would such an honor happen again. I'm an old man you see, my Elizabeth an old woman. We have no son—no child to care for us. Our lifelong sorrow. But Yahweh—blessed be His name—offered this kindness—and I will not forget. I, Zachariah, would have the honor to serve Him in His temple. That morning, I washed and dressed. I entered the chamber, the bowl of incense in my hand. I could hear the chants of the Levites. I scattered the incense over the coals—tears on my face! "Hear the prayers of Your people, Lord!"

Then suddenly—from the smoke—a voice! *"Zechariah, do not be afraid. Yahweh has heard your prayer."* Heard my prayer?

"Your wife Elizabeth will bear you a son." But how? Elizabeth is too old. I am too old! To my eternal shame, I could not believe! *"I stand in the presence of God!"* says he. *"I was sent to bring you this good news! Now because you doubted, you shall be deaf and mute until the day that these things come to pass!"*

And it was as he said. I left the Holy of Holies. I could not hear. I could not speak—until the day of his birth—when my son, John, the promise of God was born.

O Come, Emmanuel, Rejoice!

Words:
Latin Hymn

Music by
PIETRO YON
Adapted from Plainsong
Arr. by Jay Rouse

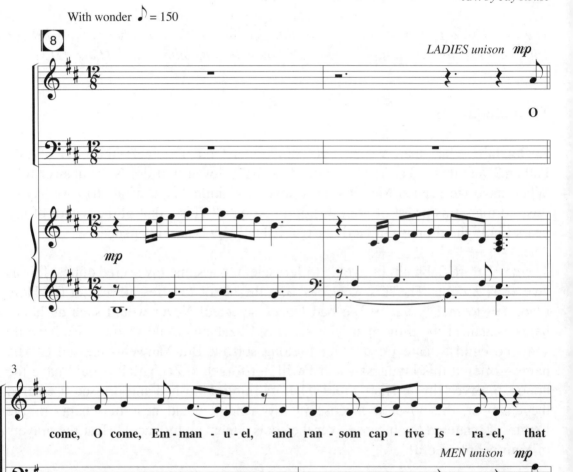

(Sopranos)

mourns in lone - ly ex - ile here un - til the Son of God ap - pear.

(Basses)

joice! Re - joice!

(Altos)
Re - joice! Re - joice! Em - man - u - el shall

(Tenors)
joice! Re - joice!

us the path of know - ledge show and cause us in its ways to go. O come, De - sire of Na - tions, bind all peo - ples in one heart and mind; bid

The Promise (optional reading):

"Do not be afraid, Mary, you have found favor with God. You will be with Child and give birth to a Son, and you are to give Him the name Jesus. He will be great and will be called the Son of the Most High..." "How will this be," Mary asked the angel, "since I am a virgin?" (Luke 1:30-32, 34)

The Fulfillment:

Mary, the Mother of Jesus: The Spirit of the most High will overshadow me? I don't understand. Am I supposed to? God's Son! I am to bear God's Son! Oh, blessed am I! Of all the women of the world, He's chosen—me! Me. Generations have longed for this promise! And I'm the one to carry it? Oh truly—truly, nothing shall be impossible with God!

I can see now how God is remembering to be merciful to the lowly—the outcast! And all history hinges on this alone—Yahweh has chosen to make a home among us—His people! He proves that He loves the forgotten. *(opt. music begins)* He rescues the helpless—the helpless. Like this Baby will be helpless. One of us! How can I bring God's Son into the world? Strange how joy mixes so easily with fear. What will tomorrow hold? I don't know—but I say yes! Yes! May the mighty hand of God do all that He wills! For God alone my soul waits. May it be to me as He has said.

Magnificat
(Mary's Song)

Words by
ROSE ASPINALL

Music by
JAY ROUSE
Arr. by Jay Rouse

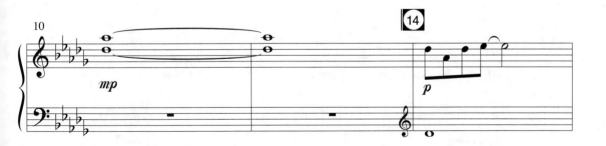

26

SOLO, gently

In my heart, a hope - ful song the an - gel sang to me. The Sav - ior of the world will come and set the cap - tives___ free! Man - y nights I

65/2096&97MD - 26

laid a - wake and won - dered at this

15

plan, this Child to be born in me, re -

mf *rit.*

deem - ing sin - ful___ man! His King - dom

rit.

28

2nd time to Coda 𝄌
(pg. 33, ms. 68) 16

comes   to us with re - demp - tion   in   His hands.

LADIES unison
mf

His

mer - cy dawns up - on   our hearts   to   all   who fear His

name. He casts the might - y from their thrones; the

MEN unison **mf**

low - ly He re - claims! Praise the God of

div.

Heav'n and earth; ho - ly is His

div.

name. His prom - ise lives for - ev - er - more; His

D.S. al CODA 𝄋
(pg. 28, ms. 33)

SOLO *mf*

His King - dom

great - ness we pro - claim!

CODA

SOLO

hands._____

He comes to us with re-

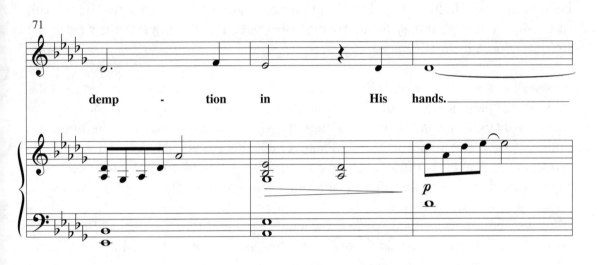

demp - tion in His hands._____

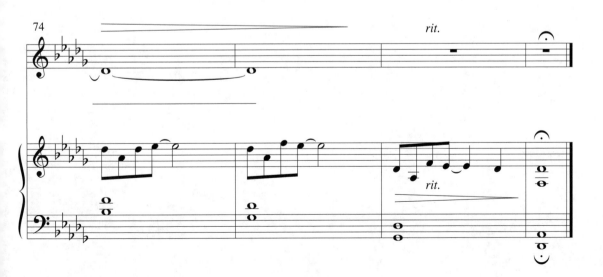

The Promise (optional reading):

But after he had considered this, an angel of the Lord appeared to him in a dream and said, "Joseph son of David, do not be afraid to take Mary home as your wife, because what is conceived in her is from the Holy Spirit. (Matthew 1:20)

The Fulfillment:

Joseph: "Jehovah increases." My name—it means, "Jehovah increases." It's never been more true. He has added blessing upon blessing. I've chosen to walk this path of obedience though it may mean my own disgrace. Still I didn't think my betrothal to Mary would bring disgrace.

Nazareth is a small village. It didn't take long for word to spread. I understood the looks—the judgment, the disappointment. But I would not—could not abandon Mary to them. Even in those first moments when I became aware something was amiss, I knew it couldn't be Mary. Whatever else happened, she didn't deserve that punishment. Maybe I couldn't ignore the hurt, but I would not put her through the public humiliation. *(opt. music begins)* This - this was the only thing I did know.

That was before the dream. Before the angel spoke His name, Jesus! Before my world turned upside-down and now I see the task, the blessing. Mary needs me. This Baby needs me. I will be His shelter. I give my word.

He Is Your Son
with **Infant Holy, Infant Lowly**
(Joseph's Song)

Words by
ROSE ASPINALL

Music by
JAY ROUSE
Arr. by Jay Rouse

INFANT HOLY, INFANT LOWLY (Traditional Polish Carol)

Babe   is   Lord   of

SOLO, freely with interpretation

I   see His ti - ny

all.

He's just bor-rowed for a - while,_____

though His feet are mine to_____ guide._____

21

_____ I'll keep Him safe and_____ warm,_____ but my

hand, watch Him grow____ each day.____

hold His hand, watch Him grow each

Ev-'ry morn-ing when He wakes, I will give Him my

day._____ When He wakes, I'll

The Promise (optional reading):

And there were shepherds living out in the fields nearby, keeping watch over their flocks at night. An angel of the Lord appeared to them, and the glory of the Lord shone around them, and they were terrified. But the angel said to them, "Do not be afraid. I bring you good news that will cause great joy for all the people. Today in the city of David a Savior has been born to you; He is the Messiah, the Lord. This will be a sign to you: You will find a Baby wrapped in cloths and lying in a manger." (Luke 2:8-12)

The Fulfillment:

Shepherd: Where should I start? Stars falling from the sky? No. Lightning? No—not lightning. Not stars. The truth is—we didn't know. But we were scared—all of us. As scared as we'd ever been. And I don't scare easily. Lions, I know. I can defend a lamb from a lion or any predator if need be—but this? This was like nothing I'd ever seen. Who'd believe us? An angel appearing in the sky isn't very believable, but a thousand of them—ten thousand? I wouldn't expect anyone to believe that. I wouldn't believe it—except that I saw it! With my own eyes, I saw it!

And as unbelievable as this sounds, most unbelievable was the message. Peace to men. His favor rests—on us! On us? You mean shepherds? We don't have anyone's favor! We're unclean. And that means one thing. We're unwelcome. It's always been that way. I suppose we're used to it. But, doesn't mean we don't know the scriptures. We do, we know the promises. And we've waited for Messiah as much as any priest. Maybe even more so. But, a stable? A manger? Messiah cannot be born in an animal's feeding trough. Maybe we misunderstood. All we knew was that we had to find out. The angel said go, and so we did! We went. And we found Him there, this Baby—this Messiah, wrapped in strips of cloth and lying in a manger.

Shepherds Run

Words by
ROSE ASPINALL

Music by
JAY ROUSE
Arr. by Jay Rouse

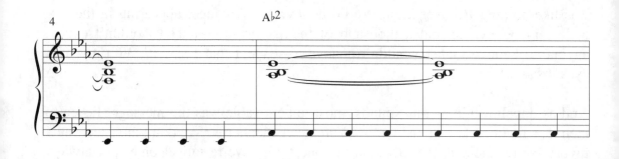

CHOIR unison
mf
Thun - der in the night sky,
A♭2
E♭2
light - ning in the hills,
God in flesh ap - pear -
A♭2
Cm7
- ing to bring to us good - will. A
D♭2
A♭

Glo - ry in___ the heav - ens.___ An - gels sing___ on high.

The stars re - flect___ their voic - es___ as

54

God is draw - ing nigh!__ Re - joice! Your King__ is com -

- ing! He's a Li - on and__ a Lamb.__ In a

man - ger He__ is wait - ing, Mes - si - ah! The

ANGELS WE HAVE HEARD ON HIGH (French Carol)

58

for ev - 'ry - one! God gives to us His Son!

The sto - ry's just be - gun!

Shep - herds, race to seek the Ba - by's face!

65/2096&97MD - 58

The Promise (optional reading)**:**

Now after Jesus was born in Bethlehem of Judea in the days of Herod the king, behold, wise men from the East came to Jerusalem, saying, "Where is He who has been born King of the Jews? For we have seen His star in the East and have come to worship Him." (Matthew 2:1-2)

The Fulfillment:

Wise Man: It was neither wealth nor influence, though I have both, that took me on this journey. I'm a scholar and an old one at that. Tired too. I've long since passed the day and desire to travel. I'm a pragmatic man of books and letters. And I would've stayed among my sacred writings—except for this; it was written! You see?! The prophetic implications were clear. I could not shake it.

The prophecies read thus. "But you, O Bethlehem…from you shall come forth for me One who is to be Ruler in Israel, whose coming forth is from of old, from ancient days. A Star shall come out of Jacob; a Scepter shall rise out of Israel." This we've studied. This we've known!

And there it was, the star of prophesy! The star of the Messiah! In the night sky! Yes, Messiah would come—and soon! One does not sit on his cushions when one encounters such a sign.

No, neither wealth nor power—but longing! This is what compelled me. And so, a journey to end all journeys! Where would it lead, we did not know. But we could not do otherwise.

We Three Kings Medley

Words and Music by
JOHN H. HOPKINS, JR.
Arr. by Jay Rouse

tra - verse a - far,

32

13 *div.*

unis.

field and foun - tain, moor and moun - tain, fol - low - ing yon - der

LADIES
16 *mf*

Born a King on Beth - le - hem's plain;

star.

Born a King on

16

mf

SING WE NOW OF CHRISTMAS (Traditional French Carol)

Pastoral Encouragement (optional reading):

Behold Jesus, the Promise. Behold Jesus, the Fulfillment. He's both—for every promise ever made finds its fulfillment in Him. Tonight we've read the scriptures, we've heard the testimony and we rejoice because the much longed for Christ has come. He was born that man no more may die.

This is more than a nice story about a baby in a manger. This is God in flesh come among us to redeem us. This is Emmanuel, God's Son, who was willing to give up His rights. So that He could become like us, He took on the very nature of a servant. Who but God would have done that? It was His choice. It was His plan, and it's what makes the gospel so amazing!

Today, we heard from Zechariah, Mary, Joseph, and the shepherds. In each of their stories we see redemption from fear and shame. We heard from the wise man who came searching and we realize that it was Jesus all along who came searching for us!

If you keep your heart and mind open, if you will be receptive to His seeking, no story of fear or shame can keep Him away. There is redemption offered for every one of us. Tonight, may the astonishing grace and humility of Jesus draw you to Himself and to His love. Amen.

Behold a Savior!

Words by
ROSE ASPINALL

Music by
JAY ROUSE
Arr. by Jay Rouse

23
God with man now
unis.
way!
now
God with man now
rec - on - ciles in a
unis.
way!
now
F
F/E♭
B♭/D
E♭
F
Gm
25
40
f
27
div.
Ba - by meek and mild.
Be - hold a Sav - ior! The
div.
E♭
Fsus
F
B♭
f
28
Son of God who comes to earth.
Be -
F
Cm
B♭/D
E♭

O HOLY NIGHT (Dwight/Adam)

Fall_____ on your knees! O hear_____ the an-gel

voic - es! O night_____ di - vine! O_____

Angels We Have Heard on High

Traditional French Carol
Arr. by Jay Rouse

89

Choral/Symphonic
Legato singing

56

Behold, A Savior! is a portrait of a promise and a portrait of the fulfillment of that promise. Throughout this musical, Jay Rouse and Rose Aspinall skillfully weave scripture and dramatic first-hand accounts of the birth of Jesus into beloved carols and original songs. Each monologue and song will take you on a journey—from the longing of Zechariah, the joy and acceptance of Mary, and the courage of Joseph to the accounts of the shepherds and wise men.

Designed with flexibility in mind, these songs and stories can be presented individually across the Advent season or in their entirety for a special event. An optional introduction and closing narration, accessible solos, and gorgeous orchestrations add to the flexibility and will make this one of the most practical collections in your library.

Companion Products

65/2096MD	SATB Score
65/2097MD	SATB Score with Performance CD
99/3922MD	Bulk Performance CDs (10-pack)
99/3919MD	Stereo Accompaniment CD
99/3920MD	Split-track Accompaniment CD
99/3921MD	SA/TB Part-dominant Rehearsal CDs (Reproducible)
30/3615MD	Full Score
30/3616MD	Set of Parts
30/3617MD	CD with Printable Parts
30/3618MD	Score and Parts plus CD with Printable Parts

Instrumentation

Flute 1 & 2	Trombone 1 & 2	String Bass
Oboe *(Soprano Sax)*	*(Tenor Sax/Baritone T.C.)*	Keyboard String
Reduction		
Clarinet 1 & 2	Trombone 3 & Tuba	Drums
Trumpet 1	Harp	Percussion 1 & 2
Trumpet 2 & 3	Violin 1 & 2	Rhythm *(Piano/Guitar/Bass)*
Horn 1 & 2 *(Alto Sax)*	Viola *(Clarinet 3)*	
	Cello *(Bass Clarinet/Bassoon)*	

Production Notes

Creating a new work has its own journey. This one is no different. As we talked through our thoughts for *Behold, A Savior!* our desire was to create a collection that would serve you in multiple ways. We wanted to provide fresh arrangements of your favorite Christmas songs, as well as give you some beautiful, new original songs.

We wanted a work that offered you the option of meaningful and accessible dramatic moments without making them intrinsic to its performance. We realized that this could be a bit of a challenge. We're happy with what developed and we hope you will be too. So, in that light...

Need music to carry you over the advent season? You'll find it in this work.

It's the first Sunday of Advent and you need a moment for the Prophesy candle during the lighting of your Advent wreath. You can easily present *O Come, Emmanuel, Rejoice!* along with the short Zechariah monologue either as a dramatic reading or with an actor in costume. There are equally appropriate moments for the Bethlehem, Shepherd candle and the Angel candle too. Maybe your time is limited and you only want to read the scripture that ties to the song. That's there for you too. You choose.

Need a whole piece to present for a special event?

This collection covers the broad sweep of the Christmas story with all its glory, as well as its most tender and intimate moments. We have provided an optional opening and closing narration for your pastor or lay person that will create a space for an altar call if you should choose to offer one.

Do you have a few good actors that would love to present a short monologue?

Adding dramatic moments without committing to a full-fledged production is easy with this workand can add another layer to your production. Monologues can be presented in Reader's Theatre fashion if you want to forego costumes and memorization.

No matter how you choose to present *Behold, A Savior!* if Christ is glorified, we will have accomplished our goal. Thank you allowing us to be part of your journey.

Jay and Rose

Some of the cover-art images and graphics from this work are available as free downloads. We hope that you can use them to assist in the making of your bulletins, posters, flyers, website and email announcements, and in any other way that's within your organization and in conjunction with performances of this work.

To access these files, please visit www.lorenz.com/downloads and navigate to the desired folder. PC users should right click and choose "Save Target As..." and Macintosh users should click and hold the link, then choose "Save Target As..." We have provided standard file formats that should be usable in most page layout or word processing software.

Due to the vast number of differences in computer system setups, we are unable to provide technical support for downloadable images/graphics by either phone or email.